# PUSH FOR PRAISE

# Push for Praise

PROPHETESS NEKESHIA GIBSON
*Sherita Gayden (front cover)*
*Mickel Gibson (back cover)*

*\*unabridged*

Superior Publishing LLC.

# Contents

| | | |
|---|---|---|
| *Preface* | | viii |
| 1 | A Familiar Place | 1 |
| 2 | Unrecognized Pain | 7 |
| 3 | Distorted Mask | 13 |
| 4 | Blind Focus | 20 |
| 5 | Forceful Tug | 27 |
| 6 | Pressed Down | 33 |
| 7 | Unfound JOY | 39 |
| 8 | Lonely Space | 46 |
| 9 | Safe Haven | 52 |

| 10 | Battle Scars | 60 |
|---|---|---|
| 11 | Escape Route | 67 |
| 12 | Soul Ties | 72 |
| 13 | Whispers | 77 |
| 14 | Missed Connection | 83 |
| 15 | Pruned Tree | 89 |
| 16 | Set Time | 95 |

DEDICATIONS

*unabridged

Copyright © 2021 by Prophetess Nekeshia Gibson

All rights reserved. No part of this book may be reproduced in any manner whatsoever without written permission except in the case of brief quotations embodied in critical articles and reviews.

Superior Publishing LLC, 2021

# Preface

Author Nekeshia Gibson

To walk with coordinated strives can potentially take you to places that are
pre-acknowledged and pre-positioned once accepted as the focal point. One will
either shoot straight for the desired stance or find different obstacles positioned
along the way to hinder progress. With many who have experience this, there is
an understanding immediately recognized of this point. But there are also those

who cannot relate due to the strain of the strives they desired to take which showed much more hurt than success. To those who have experienced that in their walk staying the course becomes a battle that resembles closely the image of war.

After that interaction with the man of God, I never broached the subject with him again. I would serve him when he sat in my section of the booth, but I did not attempt to entertain any form of conversation when I was assured, he had everything he asked for. I presumed this would let him know that I was done talking without being rude towards him. At least that was what I assumed.

Prophetess Nekeshia Gibson

# Chapter 1

# A Familiar Place

In the beginning, God separated the firmament, created the earth and all that is connected to it. From the sky to the ground, oceans to the lakes, and every speck of grass found upon it. During that time of creation, He created a version of Himself in the first living man and later woman. He gave a distinctiveness to each that reflects a difference from what they were, yet still a uniqueness unlike any other found on the earth. Separating us from each other, yet still having that one common denominator that binds us to Him forever. As time expanded, so did everyone He created. Expounding more in our differences than our actual uniqueness, lying dormant until the time our eyes are once again opened to who we truly are. Many find the answers in early periods of life and strive to see it come forth. Accepting this change without questions or hesitation. Ready and willing to move within a life that feels so welcoming from what they had previously known. Yet there are those who struggle to walk in this same direction. Not because they are hesitant or unwilling, but because their valley experience has created a view that distorted their vision from seeing the mystery, the truth. For those who walked, or continue to experience this distortion, you are not alone nor are you lost in the mist of it. Faith is the substance of things hoped for, and the evidence of things not yet seen. This is a scripture that I hold closely to my heart and one I believe I will yet see in this lifetime. Until then, I move steadily towards the God who reveals Himself increasingly in my life. It was not always this way and I do not want to give off that projection that it was. I cannot say I always lived for Him nor will I say I always served Him. I believed in Him and knew of Him, but my actions did not reflect Him in any or every aspect involving my daily lifestyle. My story is a complicated one, but it is the one given unto me to walk in. I was a mother before I was 18 years of age and still my appetite of the world had not yet been delivered from me. I still craved the attention of anyone who expressed, what I considered in those times, a sincere interest in me. Love was one thing I craved and the one thing I had yet to find. When you search for a specific something at a young age, you truly must have an accurate image of what it is and how it truly operates to implement it correctly. Without a clear demonstration or description, it can be distorted and the fruits of it will not be appealing. Creating more damage not just externally, but also internally, sadly than anything constructive or positive. The beginning of it will more than likely have the same ending, if one is lucky enough, or better yet: blessed. The projection that the mind puts before you can cause illusions of unprecedented measures and the descriptions of it will cause a distorted agreement to take place. What is love and how does it look? I have heard these questions on many occasions and never had a definitive answer; until now. Love can have so many features, emotions, descriptions, and outcome. Yet is it the actual picture? Is it the unadulterated truth? That is the question that I should have asked, but never knowing it, I continued to move in what I thought. I read so many different books and through each one I projected myself into them. Desiring a story book life where everything was practically perfect even when there were conflicts showing as well. Closing my eyes to all the darkness, pain, anguish, loneliness, and unbearable desire to just let go. Never once questioning myself to whether there was something more to what I was experiencing taking place. Desire is something else that can be explained in many ways through a fountain of words, thoughts, or actions. It is the one thing that has all these different meanings, yet it can be the one thing stolen from you if one is not careful. Looking through my eyes now, I have come to realize just how much the enemy moves to steal that part of life from you. His desire is to steal the very spark that causes one's desire of life to blossom and flourish into a mighty flame. The importance of protecting this area is so very dire to the growth and understanding that buds within a person. It is the one thing I wish I had known during those days of darkness that I may have been equipped for a greatness someday to walk in. Many days, after the birth of my first child, I walked around feeling lost, unloved, and unwanted. I gave up on myself and accepted what others thought towards me as the truth. It is true that if you listened to something long enough, you honestly begin to believe it yourself. Daily I convinced myself that nothing good would happen for me and I really did not believe my life had any form of a purpose. Before the age of 21, I was a full-blown alcoholic and had absolutely nothing going for myself. I was associated with many different people and yet close to only less than a handful. I had finally gotten my own place and it seemed as if there was a houseful each night to fill the void of what the darkness had to say. Alcohol was my breakfast, lunch, and dinner practically daily. Any form of monetary means went straight to the store for my child, nicotine and drinks. The one thing I can say, thinking back, I always had my daughter. It was painful for me to look at her knowing she deserved so much more, but I could not see me as being it. I was consumed with losing my identity and, honestly, never felt I had one. For an awfully long time, I walked around feeling faceless, as well as nameless, in a world that had not shown me anything remotely as caring. Every day I felt as if my blood were drying up on the inside and eventually, I would fade away like the sands. Even though I move daily in this loophole, I still had this flicker of hope that just would not die no matter what I endured nor experienced. I slowly began to believe the lie and live the lie in completeness. Never once questioning what or who was implementing it to the extent that it was. All I knew was it looked real, it felt real, I had been told it was real, so it had to be real. So, I thought. What truly is amazing is how many different projections a mind can inject and never loose room for more. I believe if we all had a limitation to what we insert into our thinking, our actual memory bank, we would not be as distracted with those images as we were or are. Though it is through those thoughts,those projections created about us, that cause actions and our steps to imitate what others believe as the gospel truth. After losing the will to leave this world after being unsuccessful and from the voice I could not forget, I walked around with no will for life. At that moment, I put forth every thought and words that had described me without fear or hesitation. From the moment I rose out of the bed, I instinctively completed the everyday chores I needed to do. Cooking, cleaning, ensuring my daughter was nicely put together, but my mind was focused on the time I could once again go back into the fog of forgetfulness. Once upon a time, having my own place may have been the best thing that could have happened for me and my little family. That is how it should have been, how it could have been, but it was not like that for me. It became another platform for disaster, breakdown, and rejection. Something familiarly unavoidable, but another setup for a higher authority.

# Chapter 2

# Unrecognized Pain

For some children, pain would be identified and associated with a physical incident. Whether by falling from a bike, tripping over a shoe lace, getting hit accidentally while playing, and various other ways. Mind you I said, for some children, not all. There are those children who experience pain beyond the scope of physical forms of it. Some experience the separate level of pain and associate it with the normalcy that they have endured from a tender young age. They come to believe that if it is really love, the affliction of pain renders it to be true. They do not hear the warnings coming from others and, in many cases, walk away from those that care to a doomed reality forged by their thoughts. Abusive relationships had already introduced itself into my life. It was something I had witnessed before and yet still found myself walking into the same conditions. After moving into my first place with my daughter, I had begun a relationships couple year prior to this. From the beginning, there were signs there warning me of the type of person he was, but I did not heed it. I had become use to being mistreated and physically assaulted by him at this point. His promiscuity was also part of the package as well. It is amazing to me how one can be faithful to another willing to step out even while daring you to do it. At one point in the relationship, everything became a fog in my mind. So dense that I knew I was still part of the world, but I felt myself disappearing internally. I never stopped dreaming and I never stopped knowing things before they happened. I had gotten to the point of not sharing these things with people because of the looks they would give me when things started happening. This time it was different. I remember one night waking up screaming a year or so before moving into my new home. My dream showed the same person I was dating being shot in the middle of the street. I remember waking him up and telling him what I had just saw with tears running down my eyes. After losing my closest friend not too long from that dream, the thought of losing someone else terrified me to the point I cleaved harder to this relationship. Of course, he laughed and said it was just a dream, but how could I tell him that when I dream it happens. I did not share that. I kept quiet. All I could do was silently ask whoever was listening not to allow this to happen to me. Not again. For months after that dream, I walked around afraid that it would take place.

After a while, it eventually faded from my thoughts and I was left with turmoil during that time. In between the breakups and reconciliation, my second child was born. I knew I needed to do better. I knew something needed to change, but never had the nerves to enforce this into my life. Having two young children at that point, I still barely was coping, and the abuse was still just as severe as it was from the beginning. For a while, I was unable to drink any form of alcohol and the smell of smoke was sickening. After having my second child, it was not long before alcohol came back into my life and nicotine was right along with it. During that time of blissful alcohol induced fog, the very situation I pushed to the back of my mind came forth. I remember getting ready for a house party and laughing with some of the people attending. I had already started drinking, so the fog was already forming to block everything I did not want to remember. While laughing in my semi-inebriated state, my phone ranged above the sound of the music. It is kind of funny how the sound of the phone's ring was so loud and overshadowed the music. I had one of my guests answer the call for me while I continued preparing for a fun night that looked much like every other night. I remember her calling my name while telling someone else to cut the music down. Looking at her, I knew whoever was on the other end was not someone I wanted to speak with. I took the phone and after a minute said hello. I remember hearing the other person on the line say my name and after that hearing he has been shot. The wail

I heard in my mind and heart took the breath out of me. I did not even realize that the wail I heard internally was coming out of me. I knew I needed to get to the hospital and that was the only thought that was registering for me at that moment. I eventually did get to the hospital with hope that he would be alright. I located his family and some other people with them, was told he was in emergency surgery, but there was a vibe that could not be overlooked by any of us. Not understanding what was going on, only desperate to ensure he would live, I could not let what I was feeling break my concentration of thought. I wish I could say that it stayed like that, but I would not be honest. After a while of sitting amongst the family, my friends decided to see what was going on with the behaviors towards me. I remember sitting outside on the sidewalk feeling overwhelmed by everything going on. I was doing everything I could to stop the dam in my mind from breaking and found it unreasonable hard. I knew it would not take much for the cracks to begin and pushing the bricks back into place was top priority. I looked up and saw my friend walking towards me. Looking in her face at that moment, I wanted to run away and just disappear from whatever was coming. In my mind, I knew she was coming to tell me he was no longer here, but instead her words hurt much more. After stalling for a minute, she finally told me what she had come out to tell me. I remember her asking me do I remember the people that were with his family? I gave her a puzzled look and wonder why I would want to think about that at this moment. I looked at her and realized that none of them would look me in my face. At that point I finally asked what was going on. Her next words to me were not he is gone, but these people were the family members of the woman he had become engaged to. The silence in my thoughts was more deafening than the stillness around me. The heart in my chest kept beating even though I begged it to stop. My lungs kept taking in oxygen while I still felt the effects of suffocation. The internal pain felt in that moment continue to swell even though I fought to push it down and back with everything within me. For a moment, something in my mind snapped and the oblivious feeling that came with it felt heaven sent. I sat staring at the hospital without seeing it trying with every fiber in me to understand once again why was I here? What could possibly be the reasoning behind anyone having the life I had? Was it a private joke that I was just handpicked to endure just to see how much one person could take? Was this the reality of me once upon a time dream to live day in and day out? Even with the stillness, the pause of all things around me, it was not enough to keep gravity from pulling me back down to where I was. I could hear them asking me am I alright? Before I could answer, or try to, they begin to comfort me in the way they knew how by building me up. I could hear them, appreciated it, but every word passed through me. Comfort was not a privilege I had ever experienced, and it was not coming even for that time. Pain managed to always let me know it was there and evicting it was not part of the contract it had made with me regardless of my position with it. Though this pain was different, it was not long before I realized it came to make a permanent space in cramped quarters. On the drive home, I realized that the smallest part of me I had left was still sitting on the corner at that hospital still crying with hope of relief it would not get there.

# Chapter 3

# Distorted Mask

Everyday, mirrors are used at some time in a person's life. Whether it is to do regular toiletry to prepare for the day, examine something through extra ocular resources, or simply to review what is or had been done. Either way, the view that has been established in the mind seek reassurance through this form of resources. Even though the use of a mirror can be convenient for a specific purpose, it also reflects what many do not want to see if looked at closely. It is amazing how reflections in this object can or rather will show what is also cast from the mind. The shadows of past pain, the cracks invisible to others yet visible to the one looking at them, and even the flow of tears from one who would not dare allow them to flow so freely on the surface. It is just as amazing how far a person will go to hide those issues from anyone who would see and know. It is an unwritten and unspoken law in the world that weakness cannot be allowed to show in a carnivorous world. It is simply unheard of to show strength and demonstrate weakness. To the world, that is fresh blood up for the offering and eventually the offer will be accepted. After dealing with the undeniable truth associated with a relationship that would go nowhere, I wish I could say it ended right there at that hospital. I wish I could, but that would not be honest or truthful on my part. As a matter of fact, it went on for another year before it finally came to an end and cracks were no longer the only issues I suffered. After living an alcoholic lifestyle for much of the time in my first home, I eventually moved back in with my mother. The shame and humiliation were daunting for me at this point. I eventually found employment in a restaurant and found a significant comfort in it. I had a chance to meet several different people either locally or traveling through. I soon settled in this position and loved every second of it. Each customer had a different tale to share and did not hesitate to relay things with me after seeing my interest in what they had to say. There were several customers I considered my regulars, but there was this one person who stood out. He would come in practically every morning and sit at the booth with a request for a cup of coffee while his breakfast was being made. I remember the first time I saw him getting out of his car, grabbing a newspaper, and walking in to take his seat. I did not know what it was about him, but the air around him seemed different from everyone else. Eventually I found out he was a preacher and resided at a church in the town I lived in. He would always ask howI am doing and ask about my children. Something that became a regular start to our conversation. It was kind of strange that he spoke to everyone, but always managed to talk with the cook and myself. I remember one morning he came in for his usual and we opened with the same conversation. I soon found myself asking him where he preached without thinking before it slipped out my mouth. After the question was asked, I remember thinking why I asked that, but it was too late to push it off. What stands out the most about that moment is how he smiled at me and shared how he had patiently waited for me to ask that question. I found his response peculiar and wonder why he wanted me to ask. He looked at me and told me the name of the church he pastored at with this look on his face that now resembles amusement. When I heard his answer to my question, the shocked expression made him laugh. This stranger I had just met months earlier was the pastor in the former church I attended as a child! He let me know he knew this was my family church and had wondered why I had not attended. There was no answer I could give, and I made no attempt to provide an excuse. For some reason, I knew he would know that was exactly what it would be, and my eyes disconnected in shame. The words he spoked to me next, I can still remember clearly in my thoughts. You can still come back;

do not be ashamed, everyone messes up. Before I could stop myself, the barriers slipped, and tears replaced the smile I had permanently fixed on my face. He handed me a napkin and I walked to the back. My manager asked me was I okay after seeing my face from her office. Of course, I lied and hid my feelings. I shook it off, repositioned the wall, and went back to do my job. After going back out on the floor, I saw he had gone, but left a message for me. He wanted me to know it is okay and God does not make mistakes. At that moment, I knew what he meant, but kept it to myself. How is it that this man knew so much in one sentence and had never had a lengthy conversation with me? For me, that was strange, but also scary. After that day, he did not come in for a while and my daily routine was back on course. After a while, I met someone else and moved on in the arena of relationships again. I have never looked upon race in the same aspect as others and did not see it when it came to meeting someone. He was of another ethnicity, but it was difficult to see it with his disposition. I can say that in the beginning it was a significant form of happiness and there was a difference in our relationship. Of course, being from a small town like we were, people made sure to show their thoughts behind it. For us, it did not matter, and we went about our business as if other people were not there. As time went by, we started having issues, but nothing that resembled my previous relationship. Or so I thought at the time. In this relationship, I became pregnant with my third child and that is when what was up came down quickly. Suddenly I went from being in a form of happiness to once again attempting to understand what happened. I quite my position as a waitress at the restaurant and fell into a deep depression. I could not comprehend how a sliver of happiness was so easily snatched out of my grasp right as I was closing my hand to safeguard it. The duration of my pregnancy was spent defending my name and honor from hideous lies meant to smear it. The only thing I had left was my name and I fought to keep that much of myself. After having my last child, I continued staying with my mother and eventually went back to the restaurant. Many of my old customers were still coming in and welcomed me back like a long-lost daughter. After experiencing so much coldness in my personal life, it felt like a small fire had been lit in a furnace that had long ago stop being used. I could feel myself sitting close to that flame desperately attempting to keep this small flicker of light lit. After a week or so of returning to my job, the pastor from my old church came infor breakfast. When he saw me behind the counter, a smile stretched across his face as if he had seen a long-lost friend. He gave me the biggest and warmest hug before telling me he had been praying for me. Thinking back on that moment, I now believe he passed a little strength unto me. I remember just dropping my head and wondering if the world could see my pain and my anguish that was getting just toohard to bear. Could this man see how close I was again to just simply giving up. How at that moment, I was more of a zombie than an actual person living? I gravitated to that hug and, though it lasted less than a minute, clung to the need to fill some form of hope. I honestly believe this man of God knew just how much it was needed and how it drew me away from letting go. After getting his order together, I stood speaking with him while he ate. He never picked up his paper and paid attention to everything I was saying. I remember sharing with him my very first dream as a child and the first demon I saw. For some reason, the need to share this experience with him was pressed upon me in a way I did not understand at that time. I remember he stopped eating and simply looked at me. He started asking me questions surrounding my dreams and experiences I had up until that point. After answering his questions, he continued eating and changed the subject. I did not question him to why the subject change took placed and left it the way that it was. I can remember hoping I would finally get answers to why I was seeing, hearing, and knowing the things that I did, especially the dark figure in the long black coat and hat. After he finished, he asked when I worked again. I remember telling him my days on schedule and him simply saying I will talk to you again. The look on his face was serious and I knew he was thinking on something without sharing any of his thoughts. After he left, I wondered if I had made the mistake of sharing these things that had happened to me even though it was only a small portion of events. I knew from experience how people behave towards one who says things that sound more crazy than unusual. Even though it seemed liked that to others, it never failed with situations connected to me. Everything I saw whether awake or asleep happened and each time I knew what it meant or found out later when I did not know. That night, I made up my mind once again to no longer speak on this and keep these things to myself. I would push it back again in my mind and build another wall to hold it there. Little did I know on that night, sharing my experiences with this man of God, the role he would come to play for the higher plans that were not my own.

# Chapter 4

# Blind Focus

To walk with coordinated strives can potentially take you to places that are pre-acknowledged and prepositioned once accepted as the focal point. One will either shoot straight for the desired stance or find different obstacles positioned along the way to hinder progress. With many who have experience this, there is an understanding immediately recognized of this point. But there are also those who cannot relate due to the strain of the strives they desired to take which showed much more hurt than success. To those who have experienced that in their walk staying the course becomes a battle that resembles closely the image of war. After that interaction with the man of God, I never broached the subject with him again. I would serve him when he sat in my section of the booth, but I did not attempt to entertain any form of conversation when I was assured, he had everything he asked for. I presumed this would let him know that I was done talking without being rude towards him. At least that was what I assumed. I remember one morning he came in and took his normal seat at the booth. Of course, he knew my sections and positioned himself there for me to serve him. After waiting a bit, while preparing to demonstrate the appearance of being busy, I went over to take his order. That morning, before I could posture myself to take his order, he immediately asked me was I okay. I laughed in response and said I was. His next words were a surprised to me and my mind was attempting to understand. He let me know that God wanted me to know something and asked me to come to church that Sunday or one Sunday soon. After staring at him for a moment, he then let me know he was ready to order. After taking his order, I walked back to my station and stared at him without saying a word. He never looked at me. Just sat drinking his coffee and reading his paper until his food was ready. I remember the cook turning and placing his food in front of him. I was so grateful at that moment because I did not want to go back over to serve him. I was afraid that if I went back, he would say something else and that was not what I wanted. Reading this, I can imagine the thoughts going through the minds of the readers. Why would a simple request like that cause a reaction of this magnitude from me? Well, when you have stepped so far away from the household of faith the thought of entering back in, after the things you have done, is not an easy move to make. What could God have to say to me and why did I have to go to church to hear it? It made no sense and that terrified me more than anything else I have seen, heard, or experienced. When I clocked out for that day, it was still something that weighed heavily on my mind this request made unto me. At that point in my life, I was in another relationship and had been in it for a few years. It started in a drunken state of illusion and grew to be just as blurred in abuse. I had gotten to the point of being good at hiding abuse whether physical or mental. I could laugh, joke, and entertain all in the haze of pain, fear, and depression. What is so peculiar about this state of life would be how people in the same boat gravitate towards each other with advice on what the other should do. Even though they all are dealing with one to all the same issues, each one unable to take their own advice. Now I realized that the advice was not for the one it was being positioned to, but for the one who was speaking it. Attempting to get their physical form to make the necessary move while at the same time the mind unwillingto endorse it. I desperately wanted out of it but found myself continuously going in circles with the decisions. After making it home and speaking with my children, I remember getting cleaned up to cook dinner that night. Still weighing on my thoughts were the words the man of God said to me and now I know my silence is what brought on the questioning. My new boyfriend followed me into the kitchen and sat at the table just staring at me. He begins asking me what was wrong and what happened to where I was not giving him the attention he was seeking. There was a pattern to his abuse, and I had started seeing it for what it really was. It was not that he was interested in my day or if something had happened to me per say, it was the simple fact he needed to see if anything or anyone had shifted the stance he had taken in my mind. Something he manipulated daily to ensure he did not lose his grip. I remember contemplating telling him and something wanted him to know I had been invited to church. When I looked at him and told him about it, I remember seeing his features shift for a moment. A moment long enough to see not the form of a person, but something else. Suddenly it went from just staring at me to accusing me of not being at work and "hooking" up with a married man of God. I remember looking at him in disbelief and thinking that something is wrong with this man. I did not argue with him just continued cooking my children food and ignoring what was being said to me. That night, after putting my children to bed, I laid down to get rest for the next day of work. While relaxing into sleep, I felt the pressure of a grip around my throat and opened my eyes to being choked. I remember trying to take a breath and straining with everything in me to remove this pressure from my neck. I heard the words "if I can't have you no one will" whispered in my ears before I was finally able to take a breath. I laid there in my bed, terrified and in tears, wondering why. Why did I have to continue to see days such as these with no peace or protection. It took me a minute to finally go to sleep after that. I remember thinking I was sleeping with a monster and he ensured I could not move without him knowing it. When the alarm went off that morning, I remember getting up and getting my children together for school. After getting them out the door, I was not long going out myself. I remember the relief I felt when my ride showed up running out the house from the fear that dwelled there. My coworker asked me was I alright, and of course I did not let on that anything was wrong. Being the type of person she was, she did not push me to say anything, but I knew she had left the door opened if I decided to talk. After clocking in for the day and preparing for the breakfast crowd, I attempted to stay focus on my work. Refusing to allow the night before to show on my face or disposition. What I did not realize at that time was, even though I was hiding it internally, there was evidence externally without my knowledge. As the breakfast crowd came in, I went about smiling and talking with familiar or not so familiar faces. I looked up and there was the man of God walking in to take his usual place in my section. I fixed my face, walked over to him, greeted him with his normal coffee, and prepared to take his order. He smiled as usual and began to tell me what he wanted when he stopped talking suddenly. Looking up at that point thinking he had changed his mind about his choice, I saw how his facial features were no longer the smiling featuresnormally displayed. Looking down at myself, I wanted to be sure that my shirt was not unbuttoned and revealing to my customer, especially a pastor. Giving myself a look over to check that everything was properly in place, I looked back at him curious to what was going on. After a moment, I asked was he alright, but in response he asked me was I. Confused to why he would ask me that, he pointed towards my neck and asked me again was I okay. Ashamed to have this seen and known, I positioned my collar a different way until I could go to the back. I assured him I was okay, but the look on his face hurt me to the core. It was not a look of pity nor was it a look of anger, but a look of pure sadness expressed towards me. I recognized the look and for so long wanted another person to feel what I was forever walking in. He reached out, took my hand, and placed a small white card in it. Telling me if I ever needed to talk and just want someone to listen, he was there. For a moment, I felt such a weight on my shoulders. Everything I had endured over the course of those years I sought relief, hit me like a ton of bricks. Putting the card in my apron, I asked him once again for his order before walking away to hang it up for next order prep. Walking to the bathroom, I looked at my neck and wondered how I missed it that morning. Going back out, I averted my head from the man of God. Too ashamed to even try and smile as if everything was okay. That day went by like a blur without any type of focus as I took care of my duties for the next shift. After clocking out, my coworker asked me was I ready and we walked out together to go home. While in the car, my mind was still on my shame and I could not find a voice to talk about what had took place that day. Before pulling up at my home, my coworker said my name to get my attention. I remember her saying to me it is okay to trust someone and there are good people out there. Looking at her, I could only smile as I got out of her car thanking her for the ride. I remember turning, looking up at my apartment, and thinking how did I get here again? Looking up at that moment, I did not see my life, but the illusion that abruptly was losingthe trance it had put me in.

# Chapter 5

# Forceful Tug

Examination can bring about many different revelations and perspective when it is sought. It can take place willingly and oftentimes unwillingly depending on the person. For those that seek them, it is a stance which one acknowledges the answers that comes from it. For those that experience the unwillingness of them, it places the truth before your eyes regardless of the desires to ignore. Now when it is something divinely positioned whether sought after or not, the indisputable answers can become a presence one can feel is inescapable. The latter is what I endured for a few weeks after the invitation positioned by the man of God. After a while, I could not ignore the pull that I was feeling on the inside. It became so forceful within me and would not simple be pushed to the side. The unction to go to hear what this man of God had to say was becoming an urgency I could no longer ignore or run from. I entered the process of building courage to once again enter the household of faith. It was not an easy stance and I was so very afraid to go. I remember the week that I made the decision to go that coming Sunday. I spent the entire week trying to get my clothes together and my children. I positioned the invitation to my boyfriend and was no way surprised he did not want to go. I was relieved that he was not going and happy about the decision. I know this probably sounds bad on my part, but I did not want anything hindering me hearing what I was told I would hear. I remembered when that day finally came, I got up early to fix my children breakfast before our ride came. I was excited because my coworker accepted the invitation to go as well and we were going together. I remember looking at my clothes and shoes wishing I had better things to wear. It had been a long time since I had been to church, so I did not have any up-to-date items for this. I remember my boyfriend look when he realized I was serious about going and everything he was saying/doing was not changing my mind. As a matter of fact, it made me more determine to go simply because of his reaction towards my decision. By the time our ride made it there, his disposition was so ugly that he began throwing a tantrum. I remember I looked at this man with total astonishment to how far he was going simply to keep me from going to church. I remember walking out the house and situating my children in the car. I looked up at my door and saw him standing there with the craziest look on his face. Getting into the car, my coworker asked me was everything okay while glancing up at the door. I assured her it was, told her to ignore him, and let her know I was ready when she was. On the drive there, we began to discuss where we would sit and how we did not know what to expect with this visitation. There were not any words to describe how nervous I was to enter a place I had not been in since I was a teenager. Pulling into the parking lot, a feeling of nostalgic came over me. I remember walking around to the entrance and glancing over to my grandfather's burial site. I walked over to the side of the building and glance towards my best friend's resting place as well. The pain that came over me at that moment almost took my breath away. For a split moment I almost asked my coworker to take me back home, but something stayed my voice before I could utter those words. Stepping into the waiting area, I began to twitch with nervousness and self-observation of myself. I glanced at my children and wished I had that innocence all over again towards what was happening. I remember the usher opening the door and smiling so big when she saw it was me. She reached out and hugged me while telling me under her breath how happy she was to see me. These were not strangers I was encountering for the first time. These people were my family and watched me grow up while gently removing myself from the church. I remember looking towards the pulpit and see the man of God sitting behind the podium. When he saw us coming in, he displayed the biggest grin and raised his hand towards the ceiling. In that moment, I knew he was saying something to God with that gesture of his arm. I did not know how I knew it, but I did. At that moment, I knew I had made the right decision. Finding a place in the back, we all took a seat together and nervously looked around at the heads turning to see who had just entered the sanctuary. Looking around at the people in front of us, there was a familiar face sitting a few seats ahead of me; my aunt. I remember her giving me this shocked look and then gave this little laugh letting me know she was happy to see me. The entire time I was sitting there, I became even the more self-conscious regarding my clothing and shoes. To be completely honest, I was ashamed and afraid of being ridiculed due to how outdated my attire really was. After experiencing this often throughout my young life, it was not something that did not hold potential to happen. Even though this was sitting in my thoughts, I still focused on everything taking place. Anticipating when the man of God would get up and speak to the people. I did not know if what God had to say to me would be a part of what he would present as a whole or if it would be shared with me afterwards. Once every part of the service was initiated, it was time for the man of God to come forth with the word. Sitting there, at that moment, something began to rise in my chest. For a second, it felt like nervousness, but a different kind than what I had experienced before. As the man of God preached, I could not take my eyes off him and that feeling began to expand throughout my body. At one point, I could tell he was pulling with such a force towards me. I could not explain it at that moment in my life, but now I understand a pull on my spirit was taking place with a force unprecedented. After a moment, he stopped, but that feeling inside me did not. It became so great within me to where I had to wrap my arms around my stomach to keep myself from jumping up. For a moment, he looked down at the floor, before suddenly speaking into the mic asking one of the female members to come forth with a request for a song. When she came up, he told her the song he wanted to hear her sing and let her know that he missed her singing it due to her being in the military. When she took the mic, I watched the man of God look down at the floor while closing his eyes and not saying anything. After she began to sing, the feeling within me increased in waves and crashed extremely hard against my heart. I remember the man of God starting the alter call and positioned for those who had backslid to come up. I watched as people walked up to the front and how the ushers were positioning chairs for each one. I remember thinking how full the front was with people and could feel my heart begin to weep. I wanted to go up, but I just could not take people laughing at my attire. I remember looking up at the alter again and realizing there was one chair left at the very corner of the first pew. I stared at that chair, trying to figure out how that one was empty directly in my eyesight. As if it was for me. As I sat there looking at that chair, the man of God began to pull on my spirit once again and this time he did not let up. Suddenly I started rocking and a moan flowed through me. Before I knew it, I jumped up and walked to that one chair to take a seat. When the man of God looked at me, I saw he smile and say Thank you, Jesus. While sitting there crying silently, I heard someone shouting and then felt arms wrap around me. It was my aunt. As my aunt held me in her arms, I heard her wailing in tears and it caused me to break a little bit more. I did not understand what had happened at that moment. I only knew that, at that time, I could not hide my pain. For a moment, just for a brief second, I let the tug pull out what was being held in on that day.

# Chapter 6

# Pressed Down

Shadows have the tendency to project offany solid mass or object that stands within any form of light. What is even the more interesting about shadows would be that it does not take a certain amount of light for it to form. Whether engulfed in a large amount of light or barely a substantial amount, shadows always find a way to project off its designated point. Another interesting features to shadows would be they are not always connected to something or someone. When you look around, shadows perform according to their own means of when or how. These are the shadows that many dealswith and avoid interacting with primarily for what they can have hidden. When something is out of sight it does not always mean it is out of mind. It could simply be placed in a location one avoids,eliminating what comes about from acknowledging it. With that being the case, shadows take on a life from this situation. They wrap around the hidden and wait with patience. Lurking, lingering, waiting for that opportune moment to remind you, it is still there with no intentions of leaving. After my experience at church, I felt a release from the weight I had packed on over the course of time. It was a freedom that one who has been stuck in a cage waiting for someone to come along and open the door. Open it just enough to see that I can walk out without fear or hesitation. Giving just enough hope to once again believe in possibilities regardless of the flaws my mind associated with this feeling or thought. I remember that this feeling stayed for several weeks and there was a shift taking place along with it. My boyfriend saw this change as well, but it did not matter to me. I was no longer sitting isolated from depression, misery, and loneliness. I felt a stirring within, and I began to hunger for a better life than what I was currently living in. This also was felt concerning my children. I did not stop going to church after that first encounter. Over the next few weeks, I found myself going to the clothing store purchasing new items for my children and myself. I was not at a place to where I could buy a lot of things or too expensive things, but it felt good to have better things. I could tell my boyfriend was not too happy with my "sudden" willingness to draw closer to The Lord. As a matter of fact, he would do things trying to prevent me from going, but I would ignore him through it all. I remember one week, closer to the weekend, I took an overnight shift to earn a little more money to go buy more things for myself and my children. After getting off that morning, I came home to a quiet apartment from everyone still being asleep, placed my tips on the dresser, bathe, and fell into bed. I remember smiling a slight smile because in a few hours my children and I would be getting more clothes. It just felt so good to see clothes being built up for church and not parties. I remember waking up and hearing the tv in the living room playing. I knew it was time to get up to avoid losing sleep that night for Sunday morning. I got up, did my routine stretch, and prepared for a long sleepy day. I remember slowly walking to the foot of the bed to grab my house shoes and robe. I glanced over at the dresser and noticed my tip money was not there. Confused, I walked closer to the dresser to be sure I did not put it in a different place. After not seeing it, I decided to check my apron to see if I could have possibly left it in there while thinking I put it on the dresser. After checking it, I began to panic! At that point, I was going through my uniform hoping with everything in me it was in there. It was not. I remember standing there trying to think where my money could have gone and not having a clue. Form a moment, I tried to ignore that nagging thought and the feeling rising in my gut. No, it could not be true. Just was not possible. That is when I had a clear vision, like a movie, play right before my eyes. When it began to play, sound came along with it to illustrate what I was seeing. I saw my boyfriend slowly getting out the bed in an attempt not to wake me. I saw him walk over to the dresser, pick up my money while watching me, ball up the paper I had on top of it, and slowly open the door while being sure I did not wake up from his actions. I saw the look on his face and realized that it was pure hatefulness. I heard his thoughts and knew he was attempting to stop me from going back to church. After snapping out of it, I said that was crazy he would not do something so lowdown to me regardless of his behavior. I had to believe he was in the front room, with my children, allowing me to sleep from a long night at work. I desperately needed to believe this because the money was not just for church, but also a bill that needed to be paid by Monday morning. Opening my bedroom door and walking up the hallway, I found my children watching Saturday morning cartoons while eating cereal. I did not fuss at them for their bowls being on the floor. All that was on my mind was seeing if this man werethere to eliminate the feeling that would not go away. After looking in the living room, kitchen, and going back to check the restroom, I walked back into the living room slowly. I looked at my eldest child and asked her did she know where he was. She told me he had left after fixing them cereal a long time ago. At that point, all the strength I had been gaining left every inch of my body. My mind was so stunned with disbelief that this person, who occupied my home, had taken every dollar I had to my name. I remember my oldest looking at me and I knew I had to fix my face. My children, even at a young age, could tell how I was feeling, and I did not want them seeing this. I smiled, went into the bedroom to put some clothes on. I went into the kitchen to prepare them some lunch while moving in a daze. As the day went by, I waited with anger growing steadily and profoundly within me. I remember going in the bedroom, while my children were eating dinner, and putting everything this man own in a trash bag. I sat everything at the front door knowing as soon as he stepped into the door, he would see it. With hopes it would trip him up. When my front door open, I had just prepared my children to go with my mom for the night. I was hurt, angry, and tired from this day I had faced. My plans were no longer for church, but to do extra hours to get the money needed for the bill that had to be paid. I was not going, but I still wanted my kids to go and I did not want them home. He would not be there, and I would be at work. I am glad I made the decision to send them with my mom. After walking into the house, I remember seeing him look down at his stuff. He began to question me to why it was there, but only met with a question of my own. After looking at me with this weird expression, he gave this response like he had no idea of what I was talking about. I asked again with the stance that I already knew the truth. His response was to laugh in my face and then called me crazy. At that point, there was no hesitation in my thoughts that he had to leave. I remember telling him to get his things and leave. At that point, his demeanor shifted, and his stance became almost predatorial. I remember him walking up to me and letting me know he was not going anywhere causing me to become infuriated. Thinking back on that moment, I realized now there were signs there to what was about to happen. I remember walking around him, grabbing one bag, and moving to toss it out the door. The next thing I knew, I hit the floor which caused my head to bounce from the impact. Trying to collect my thoughts, he pounced on me with his hand around my throat and the other one hitting me. I remember looking into this man's eyes and seeing a crazed, glossy, wild look staring back at me no longer looking human. After getting away from him, I cowered beside the coach. I remember him walking into the bathroom, taking a shower, and then going into the bedroom. I sat there, afraid and alone, in every sense of the words. The sense of freedom was gone and once again the cage felt closed. Where there was once hope for new beginnings had been replaced by endless traps with no means of escape. At least not for me.

## Chapter 7

# Unfound JOY

Happiness is a rightful experience and inheritance to anyone no matter who they are. It is amuch sought after feeling and fulfilling when it is experienced. With this- feeling, the emotion of joy develops from it. An under- line emotion that causes one to bubble over with the desire to see everyone encounter it and walk in it. It is not always an easy emotion to gain and not always an easy one to keep. With each day of holding it, one can find themselves fighting to keep it despite what comes their way. Though this word is in much reading mater- ial and relevant for those who continually walk in it; the same cannot always be stated for obtaining it. Life can be funny in this area for many and cause them to envy the few with it.Envy was the emotion I steadily walked in when I saw joy on the face of others. It felt as if I was denied this one emotion even when I got a small bit of happiness. Joy was not something that came my way, so I could not describe this emotion. Despite everything I could possibly do, it took much for me to even experience a steady stream of happiness much less joy. After that night of building my confidence up to walk away from abuse, I pushed that thought away for fear. It became my blanket of comfort and, once again, alcohol became my nurse. I lost focus on the changes that were coming forth bringing the much-needed improvement. The thought of the freedom that was at the tip of my fingers became too painful to even ponder over, so I pushed them to the back of my mind. It made no sense to consider it as an option. I felt trapped, accepted being trapped, and slowly adapted to that position. It is true that every abuser is different and each one operates with certain knowledge. They enter a relationship with a party, examining where that person is in their minds, find a vulnerability, and launch the ultimate claim to possess them. Once they do this, the person is nolonger a human being to them, but a possession. Now depending on what level, the abuser is on makes a big different. You have the novice that islearning the rope, the moderate who has developed to a comfortable place, and the pro. The pro is the one who finds pleasure in humiliating, breaking, terrifying, and overtaking another human being or rather weaker species. Their main purpose is to enslave the mind of a person and draw them away from anything that would build them to be stronger than they realized they were. They know what to say and how to say it to ensure they do not loose what they had trained to be obedient to them from studying. Once you connect with a pro, they are not always human any longer. A lot of times they have been overtaken by something not human. Do not take me wrong, sometimes pros can just be evil flesh with a taste for inflicting pain on another person. That is true, but there are those who do it with a demonic intent and do not mind you knowing. That is what I, unfortunately, had connected with. I remember a few weeks after that horrible night being so afraid to even speak to anyone. Even with my customers which they came to notice. The cheerful energetic young lady now resembled a shell of who she had shown to other people. I remember one morning, while at work, the man of God came in for his normal breakfast. I knew it had been a couple weeks since he had come in, but I did not broach the subject because I had not been back to church after that weekend of abuse. I remember going over to where he sat, acknowledging him, and positioned to take his order. That morning he only wanted coffee and I did not question his limited choice. In my mind, the less I asked the less he would as well. I remember walking back and placing his coffee, water, and creamer in front of him. Giving a slight smile, I dropped my eyes, and turned prepared to walk away until a refill was needed. I had gotten to the point where I begin to look down more and more. To me, it was a way to hide my eyes, but also the weight of what I was dealing with was just too much to stand upright. Before I could take a step, the man of God said my name loud enough for me to hear. I turned back thinking he may have changed his mind, but unfortunately that was not the case. He began by asking me how I was doing and was I alright. Of course, I told him I was great, and everything was good plastering a small smile on my face. I could tell by the look he gave that he did not believe me but did not push for the actual truth. I really appreciated that. He then told me how he had miss seeing me at church since the last he saw me and of course I fabricated a story as a reason. I could not expose my shame and the fear I had come to settle in after that weekend. I knew by the look he gave me he knew everything I was saying was not the truth. It also felt as if he knew what was going on but wanted me to be open with him. This was not something I could do with anyone. Trust was not a part of who I was during those time and for me, everyone had an agenda. He then started sharing with me the sermons he had preached since the last time I had attended. I listen to what he was saying and felt the urge to grab everything he was willing to share. I did ask a few questions regarding certain points he shared with me to get more understanding to what he was saying, and I could tell this pleased him to hear my curiosity. After a while, I asked if he would like a refill, but he turned it down letting me know he was preparing to leave. The next part of the conversation is replaying over my thoughts even as I prepare to write it. After drinking the last bit of his coffee, the man of God informed me he was leaving. He let me know he was no longer at my former church and had hoped to see me before he left. I remember standing there staring at him in complete disbelief. All that kept playing over and over in my thoughts was "not again". I remember him asking me would I promise to keep going to church regardless no matter what. I remember telling him, while looking him in the face, no I would not. I could see he was not happy with my response and proceeded to explain how this was important for me. At that moment, I lost whatever little bit of stance I had tried to hold on. It seemed as if no matter who or what comes into my life, everyone eventually left me. I believe he saw in that moment I was unreachable and had closed myself off from listening. I remember him asking if I still had his card and I instinctively reached into my apron pocket pulling it out. Until this day, I do not know how I kept that in my pocket with the many times I had to wash my apron from use. He let me know that if I ever needed to talk to not hesitate to call and I nodded in acknowledgement. Saying goodbye, I watched this customer who was once mysterious to me become a lifeline walk out the restaurant for the last time. I remember my thoughts forming in a dark area throughout my mind. The little glimmer of hope, sliver of light, was now no longer glowing in any form or fashion. I remember pushing back tears and holding down hope. Walking in the life I had experience so far was daily showing itself to be permanent. Nothing would change and I was starting to accept it. Who was I kidding? Myself? This was the life I was given; the life I was assured I would not escape, and it was time I accepted it for what it was. I remember finishing my shift and going home or what had become my jail for the day. Preparing my children and boyfriend's meal for them before preparing them for school the next day. I remember how focused my boyfriend was on my every move and every step I was taking. He had already completed the "I am sorry" routine, but he knew like I knew it was not real or sincere. He began asking me what was wrong and why was I not saying anything. At that point, it did not really matter if he knew or not, so I told him what happened. I remember he laughed out loud causing me to look up at him wondering what he felt was so funny. He looked at me laughing and said, "well I guess you won't be going back to that church huh." The way I felt at that moment was numbness with no warmth or feeling. I looked at this person in front of me laughing and felt complete dislike. I knew from the way he was laughing and prior behavior he never wanted me to go to church either way. Walking out the room, I remember going into the bedroom to sit on the end of my bed just simply staring at the floor. Mind you, I have already shared that my eyes always were looking down at the floor. Now I understand that the reason behind this was because I did not feel that anything above that point was worth looking at. The only special thing in my life, that I could see during that time, were my children and that was it. Even then, I did not feel that I had the right to look upon them. Every hope, every dream, every desire, and, for that moment, every friend,I had managed to truly consider to be that were gone. In its place was misery, fear, pain, and emptiness. This was a place that continuously reminded me it had taken up residence without any plans to move without giving me permission to ask. God, what kind of life had you given me was the question I asked to the voice who did not answer at that time and remained silent.

# Chapter 8

# Lonely Space

The mind is a wondrous organ that controls in many aspect the entire body's functions. Once the mind stops sending signals to areas within the body, the body will stop due to instructions no longer coming forth. When signals stop without cause or reasoning, it takes a specialist to examine then explain what has happened to cause the signaling cancellation. Now though one may not be a "specialist" to why something is happening, they are yet consciously aware that there is an issue going on in that area not functioning correctly. One thing that a person tends to do when something is going on would be discussing it with another to possibly get an idea or theory to the problem. That is once it is consciously acknowledged to be examined first by the one who is experiencing the issue, but there is another platform that goes with this same concept. There are those who deal with signal loss but have become too numb to even consider there is something seriously wrong going on. That much should be looked at, acknowledged, and examined to determine how it had been allowed to continue. Not considering the repercussions that will eventually take place if it is not moved on. This is where I found myself not long after the man of God left. The signals that once would come to cause me to look around at the areas surrounding me were no longer present. Where I once would review what I am thinking or seeing in front of me became a blur of nothingness. A complete numbness had moved into its place and I could care less about asking it to go away. For me, that was an ambrosial welcomed to avoid examining anything that would cause feelings and emotions to come forth in this shell I was trapped in. I continued my everyday activity of work and home without thoughts, feelings, or emotions. After a few months, I ended up leaving my small town and moving to a different area in the state with my boyfriend. I had suffered weight loss, completely lost inner, and hopeless for anything or one better. I left my children with my mother and everything I had behind. I allowed this man to convince me to go with him to this nicer place around people connected to him, but no family of my own. I remember getting there and thinking maybe this would be better than where we were. Is it possible that with the change of environment things would get better for us, but even more for myself? It broke something inside of me to leave my babies behind, but my mind state was still they have a better chance of doing much more than with me. I was completely convinced of this. I was told that we had a house on the spot, and it was ready for us to move right in apart from a few things that needed to be done. I had a small portion of excitement that was forming inside of me and just a little desire that this would be a good move for us. I remember on the ride to this new home thinking about how I would fix up the kids' room and surprise them once we got on our feet. I set a three-month deadline to get my kids and bring them to be with me. Even though I felt unworthy of being their mother, I still could not deal with not being with them. The only warmth I had experienced so far came from them and it was becoming unbearably cold without them being near. I remember we pulled up to this new place and I became even more excited. It was huge on the outside and looked nice from what I could tell due to it being night. I remember grabbing my bags and standing with a mixed feeling of excitement. This did not last long. Once we walked in, and the lights came on, my eyes took in what was positioned to be a good opportunity. I remember looking around in a frozen state and realizing I had been lied too again. I know you are thinking this is not a surprised but mind you when you are living a life outside of God, you do not realize that the world takes more than it will ever give. I believe my facial expression must have shown what I was thinking because an explanation was given to me. Whereas I was under the impression that this new house in a new town was given to us with the understanding of rent payment offset until jobs were obtained; I was now being told it was agreed to that we, meaning myself and boyfriend, would work on the house in addition to paying rent. Hearing this agreement, I felt anger rise for the first time in a long time over the numbness that had become the more normal feeling. I remember my boyfriend interrupting the conversation before I could say anything and basically agreeing that I already knew this, which was a lie. I remember walking around this house and being in complete shock. The basic utilities were missing in the kitchen with the promise of it being different before the week ended. I remember sitting down on a bucket in the living room and just staring at the floor. While this person I allowed to convince me to leave everything I had laughed and joked like nothing was wrong. After our ride left, the mood changed from laughing to accusation of being ungrateful. I remember looking at this man and simply wondering if there is anything human within him. After a while, I remember going to the bedroom and was so happy to see a fresh bed in the house. The only thing on my mind was sleep and thoughts on what was I going to do? Every dollar I had was used for this bus ride to this town for a so-called fresh start. Only to find out it was not a fresh start, but a lie wrapped up to look like a beginning for what was surely going to be an ending. Contemplating in my head the thoughts swirling around, I remember my boyfriend talking aimlessly with attempts to lighten what he had done. I remember his continuous words and his eyes studying me trying to determine my thoughts or get a reaction. I did not give him what he wanted. I remember looking at him while he made these exaggerating comments towards the house, his "fresh start", our relationship, but never once bringing up the fact he lied or this agreement he made for "us". Looking at him at that point was not an easy thing to do. I felt myself moving towards a place where the sight of him was making me physically ill and hearing his voice was a strain on my nerves. I felt the cork on that bottle inside me slowly moving up and the old glue put around the edges starting to crack as it turned ever so slightly. As I laid down, exhausted from the ride and the information I had just learned, I stared up at the ceiling with acknowledgement that this step was just as bad as many others I took. I was still this gullible, love seeking, hopeful, fool who fell for a lie I knew was one when I heard it. Truth was not part of his vocabulary and it was rubbing off on me when people would bring him up to me. I would find myself saying untrue things about him or us because of the embarrassment of being with someone like this. I remember him still talking away and me completely blocking him out. Ignoring his words and simply turning my back with no comments and as a sign the conversation was just not there for me nor was it on my mind. I remember feeling him sit down on the bed, quiet at that point, and I knew without turning he was staring at me with the realization his words meant absolutely nothing. I was in an entirely different area away from my children and family. With no one, but this man and people connected to him that only he knew. The isolation was unbearable, and it is a sign of what is, not would, come from a person like this. Abusers like to do their handiwork in isolation and, sometimes, amongst familiar sources. Their goal is to completely shatter whatever may be left of spirit, fight, and defiance on any level. I considered this move I made to be the loneliest place right then. I had no idea the horror and terror that was to come from within.

# Chapter 9

# Safe Haven

Security is the one thing that everyone expects to experience in some shape, form, or fashion. It is not always promised, but it is yet still wanted. In many cases, unfortunately, it is needed. For some, safety is experienced at a young age and carried over into adulthood. Which inspires them to recreate the same effects for their love ones. For others, safety is a wishful experience that they neither had growing up and have no way of identifying what it looks like in the adult arena of life. It is explained to them through school, conversations, or possibly television, but not demonstrated through the life they have lived. There are those who had experience a form of safety growing up and become lost during the evolving of adulthood. The perception of it changes because of other issues or experiences they have endured in the transformation. With that being the case, the distortion causes the images to lose strength and relevance in the position it once had. This is where I found myself at this point of time. I was no longer in my comfort zone and there was no one to whom I could turn to for help. At least that is what I assumed. After a couple weeks of being in this new town, I did manage to acquire a new job in a decentplace. It was associated with customer service and it correlated with what I have come to learn from the restaurant business. I remember the excitement of starting a new field and learning a different area of customer service. The one thing that made me nervous was not the new position, but the new manager I would be working under. He was this big hulking man who was formerly military and carried a look that could cause a grown person to cringe when he looked at you. He did not speak much, but when he did it was as if his eyes pierced through you to see the answer before it was provided. I was incredibly nervous to be around him, but I felt safe with him. Sounds strange I know, but there was a protectiveness about him that I felt with my grandfather. I remember starting this new job and I jumped every time he said something to me. I remember the look he would give me when I did this, but he did not address it only continued speaking or whatever it was that caused him to get my attention. Eventually he placed me on day shift, and I believe, until this day, it was a deliberate move for my benefit. I say that because being in a new town with only people known by one sided relationship can be a trying time for a person. There were promises made that sounded like people will be there to help you, but eventually people let you know by their actions and/or words how they really felt. I remember one time getting off in the evening hours and having to sit for a couple hours waiting on a promised ride. After a while, my manager came outside with an offer to take me home due to him watching to see how long I was outside. I remember being ashamed and having no other option but to accept the ride. I was considering the outcome of coming home in a car with another man and having to defend my actions with what was at the house. For the first time, I am admitting that this house I was occupying was not my home, but a shell that I stayed in reflecting how I had been feeling for as long as I could remember. It looked nice on the outside, but the inside was empty practically bare. That was me in more ways than one. I remember jumping out of my manager's car without him barely coming to a complete stop. I said thank you, but before I could turn, he spoke my name to gain my attention. Turning to acknowledge I heard him, my manager asked me a question with that same look as if he already knew the answer without me saying anything. When I heard the question, I was completely shocked, and my face had to have answered before I could respond. He asked me was I being abused at home? I remember the look he gave me as he waited for my verbal comment though he had received a facial response. I remember shaking myself and giving a small laugh while telling him no. I could not get myself to say anything more than that and honestly, glad I did not. I knew he would not believe me and the look on his face let me know he was not fooled by my answer. I remember him nodding his head in response to my answer and telling me if I ever needed help, he was there. I looked at this big man with this strong face and could not believe the sincerity coming from him nor his tone. I realized at that point that he recognized the signs and was offering to help. Where I was at that point was terrified of what I was living with. A small part of me wanted to accept this man's help, but the fearful part of me believed my boyfriend would still get to me some way. Plus, I was a long way from home, so help was not close regardless of how it was positioned by others. I remember seeing him look towards the house and turning I saw my boyfriend standing in the door looking. I turned back, told my manager thank you for the ride, and closing the door to walk towards the house. Walking past my boyfriend into the house, I turned to see my manager still sitting there looking at him before pulling off. I walked to the kitchen to look in the small refrigeratorfor something to eat. Mind you, coming to this "new opportunity" was nowherebeneficial nor had any "promises" given held up. Food was scarce and help was even scarcer. I believe I lost right at 15lbs. after this move due to the exaggerated information, I had been given by all parties involved. I heard the front door closed, and shutting my eyes, prepared for a battle. I knew this was going to be this way because of all the beer and liquor bottles that were on the counter.

This also let me know that my boyfriend had literally sat around the house all day watching television while drinking. Walking into the kitchen, I remember him leaning against the doorframe and asking me who this man was that brought me home. Taking a deep breath, after hearing the level of alcohol in his voice, I let him know this was my manager. Questioning how I managed to get home by him, I let my boyfriend know that the help positioned by those connected to him was just as empty as this house we were living in. The next thing he said floored me and I remember staring at him as if I really did not know who he was. Looking at me, my boyfriend informed him that the person who was supposed to pick me up called to let him know I was not at work over two hours ago. I remember him taking a step towards me, with another one of his beer bottles in his hand and repeating again his question. I remember looking at him and anger rising inside of me for this blatant lie that had been placed on me. I could not tell if it was a lie said to him or if he was just making something up in his drunken state. He was a big liar and rarely spoke the truth. At that point, it did not matter to me which was which when it was me doing everything. I remember standing my ground and looking this drunken person in the eyes without any form of fear. I remember telling him that was a lie, and he could believe whatever he wanted as far as I was concern. I walked past him at this point without looking back to enter the bathroom to prepare for the next day. While in the bathroom,

I heard the front door close and was grateful for a few minutes of peace. After coming out the bathroom, I remember going back to the kitchen and making myself a sandwich before going to bed. I do not remember falling asleep, but I do remember jumping up in the bed due to this loud noise that came from the front of the house. I reached beside me to shake my boyfriend and realized he was not there. I got up, went into the kitchen to grab a knife while looking around in the dark to ensure no one had broken in while I was asleep. After seeing no one in the house, I remember walking to the window and glancing outside to determine whether someone was possible out there. I had gotten to the point where I was used to my boyfriend not coming home for days after leaving drunk. Looking outside, I saw something lying on the ground in the yard and realized it was a person. Fear rose in me and all I could think was someone had killed my boyfriend leaving his body in the yard. Never once did I consider it was someone else, but this person I had come to feel I was stuck with. I remember running outside and calling his name after realizing that it was truly him. He moved and I helped him get up to make it into the house to get him off the wet grass. Smelling the level of alcohol on him, I could not believe that anyone could smell totally like what they had consumed. Angry, I slammed the door closed after dropping him on the floor without any pity to whether he would catch himself in the process. I remember turning seeing him sitting up halfway on the floor barely able to stabilize himself. I remember thinking with disgust how I long to be away from him and turned to walk pass him to get more sleep before work. Right when I walked past him, I felt his hand wrap around my ankle, and snatch my legs out from under me. I remember hitting the floor on my stomach and feeling this man climb on my back to put me in a choke hold with all his strength. In that moment, I felt the limited amount of air going into my lungs and the strain of his muscles under my hands as he squeezed a life that he did not hold valuable in that moment. I remember getting strength and pushing with all my might to break free of his grasp. At one point of time, he began to hit me across my temple and head causing me to be stunned while fighting back. Breaking free, I remember him grabbing me again and this time slamming me on my back while sitting on me with his entire weight squeezing my neck in the process. Looking him in the face, I did not see a human being, but a monster with every intent of taking my life while smiling as he did it. I remember thinking, Lord help me, and fought to free my breath from the grasp of my enemy at this point. I remember some way, somehow, getting free, and seeing him lying on his back after falling backwards. Until this day, I cannot explain how this happened, but I took that opportunity to run to the bedroom and lock myself in for the remainder of the night.

Terrified of what stood on the other side of this door and unwilling to allow it access again. That night, I realized I had to decide. I had to make a change. It was no longer a matter of fighting for survival, I was now fighting for a life I did not think I still wanted. What stood on the otherside of that door represented the very thing that had desired to see me disappear as if I had never existed at all.

# Chapter 10

# Battle Scars

Every warrior does not come out of a conflict without some form of proof that he or she has participated in one. Whether it is through the mental strain of enduring or through a physical brand, there is always some kind of mark left to testify that this person came through. Though it is not always evident to the eye the amount of inner damage inflicted through the scars not always seen on the surface. In order to see that, one must have a microscopic lens to conduct this form of analysis to determine the depth of the tear. In many cases, it is not always the length of the scar that causes the most pain, but the depth of the wound when it takes place. All scars cannot be seen, but they most definitely can be felt to a capacity that can be mined blowing. After enduring the night before, I did not want to be in the same house as this man. The terror of how close I came to losing my life at the hands of this man was too uncomfortable to stay in the same space. I remember getting up and preparing for work the next morning with an urgency. I was very watchful when locking the restroom and bedroom doors to ensure what was in him could not get to me while I was getting ready. I remember grabbing my purse and shoes then practically running out the front door to wait on my cab. I had no intentions of trusting on the ride that was too fickle towards their agreement of assistance. Plus, I did not want anything to cause me to have to spend the day at home due to this unsteady agreement, so I called to ensure I had a way to get out of this house. Sprinting through the house, I saw my boyfriend lying in a drunken heap on the floor not far from where he had fell the night before. If I could be real in just this one moment, I did not care if he were breathing, hurt, or simply unconscious at this point. I remember the relief that washed over me when the cab pulled up to the house and my haste to get in. I looked back at the house and in so many ways wished I did not have to see that place again. My heart had desired so greatly to see one hope, one action, or at least one move be better than any of the things that had taken place so far. But in less than a blink of an eye, I was seeing just how little life had yet to offer me. I remember getting to work and sitting on the sidewalk waiting for my manager to show up. Looking at the time, it did not dawn on me just how early I had arrived to get away from the monster residing in the house. Realizing I had right at an hour to go before the store opened, I had nothing to distract me from going into my thoughts. The one place I seldom want to visit because it never had anything worthwhile to review. I remember thinking over various points in my life and how each one just brought on worthless emotions. All I could see was steps moving slowly downward with little promises of going up. I was so caught up in my thoughts that I did not see the car turn into the parking lot until it got right up on me. Turning to see who could be coming this early in the morning and realizing it was my manager. Getting up, I paste a smile on my face and presented the mask I had been wearing for so many years to the world. As stated before, to give the impression of strength and show weakness in a carnivorous world could not be done. So, I presented what I knew to be a safety net to avoid being tried in other areas. A rage was building up within me and I was fighting with everything in me to pushed that down and strip it of the damage I knew it could bring. I remember watching my manager walk up to me and the look over he was giving me while approaching. There was little doubt he was seeking to see if anything had happened after he dropped me off the day before. In my mind, I was glad I had positioned my clothes to where the evidence could not be seen. I also applied makeup to my face, especially my cheek and neck to lessen the tale telling bruising that were trying to form. There was nothing I could do about the swelling, so I had worn a long wig to try and hide that much. Fixing it so that it fell mainly over that side to where it was not noticeable if it was really looked at. It seemed as if it was working because my manager did not say anything to me about my looks. I was so relieved to the point I was genuinely able to smile as he unlocked the store doors to go in. He did not even inquire to why I was there so early, and I did not dare ask him the same. I knew if I had it would open the door for him searching to see what my response would be towards the same question. That was the one thing I did not want to take place due to the emotionally state I was still trying to push behind the brick wall in my mind. Walking into the store, I remember him telling me he wanted me to take the lead for the day. I did not mind this because it meant I would be free from personal thoughts for a few hours. Walking over to my cash register, I placed my personal items in the space available for that purpose while waiting for my manager to bring my cash tray to prep for the morning service. Leaning against the backdrop of the register, I looked out the store windows watching traffic moving in its normal rush hour that people took to get to their destinations that morning. I remember hearing my manager coming out of the office and turning to watch him bring the cash tray. He was looking down at it while walking towards me explaining to me how he wanted me to count the tray to determine if I had enough change. Agreeing to what was being asked of me, he glanced up at that point to hand me the tray for me to do what he asked. I remember turning to put the tray in the register and begin to count the money as directed. When I finished, I let him know I should be okay and looked back at him with a smile. I remember the expression on my manager's face and realized this was not the normal look he always had. His face was red, and his jaws were so tight to where you could see where the bones connected in his head. He did not say a word, just turned and walked away leaving me standing wondering what had just happened. After the store opened and the morning crew came in, everything was going as usual. The only difference was my manager stayed in the office and did not come out for a couple hours. I remember wondering if he would eventually do his normal walk through but did not have the nerves to go ask. Right when I was pondering that thought, my manager came out the office, informed the second register he would be back in an hour, and left without saying anything else. I remember watching him get into his car and drive off as if he were in a hurry to get somewhere. After an hour, my manager pulled back up, walked into the store, asked if everything had been smoothed, and went into his office closing the door. Watching him, I could tell his mood was slightly different and did not realize what was about to take place. Not long after returning, I remember my manager coming to the door asking me to step into the office. Worried, I started wondering if I had done something wrong due to the attitude his voice carried and prepared for the worst. Walking into the office, I closed the door behind me as instructed, and sat down in the chair across from him. The first question out of his mouth had nothing to do with the store or anything regarding the store. Looking me in my eyes, my manager asked if I needed help? Shocked, I remember looking at this man who only met me through the interviewing process of a job, and now was positioning a way of escape. In that moment, I could not laugh nor could I pretend any longer. A hammer hit my wall and a crack came from it. The force was so great to where it did not give me time to pretend, lie, or hide behind either of them. I remember how the words would just not form and when I managed to open my mouth, all that came out was the breath I held. I remember dropping my head and silent tears rolled down my face unto my lap. My manager sat for a moment silently watching me and I truly appreciated that. Finally, he repeated his question and I let him know thank you, but no. For some reason I still could not separate myself from the grips this man had on me. I remember my manager saying he knew I would say this and until I was ready, it was my choice. Leaning up on his desk, I remember my manager looking me in my eyes and asked me do I remember him leaving. Puzzled and wondering what this had to do with the conversation, I told him of course. He had just returned prior to calling me into the office and I found that question odd. Still looking at me, my manager simply said, "you do not have to worry about him putting his hands on you ever again." Staring at him, I remember thinking this man was serious and telling me the truth. I knew that there was a connection between his leaving and this conversation. I remember the phone to the store ringing and my manager reaching over to answer it as if it was a normal conversation. I remember watching him and him stretching his arm towards me while saying the call was for me. Taking the phone, saying hello, I heard my boyfriend's voice on the other end. He asked me what time I was getting off and began to apologize in a way that had a different tone towards it. Listening to what was being stated on the phone, I glanced at my manager as he silently looked at papers on his desk while listening to a one-sided conversation. Hanging up the phone, my manager let me know I could have the rest of the day off and the next if I wanted. I remember acknowledging his comments and calling a cab to pick me up. Once I made it home, I remember walking in and my boyfriend and his relative were sitting in the house talking. When he saw me, his entire attitude was different, and it was as if nothing had ever happened. That horrible night was the last time he put his hands on me and until this day, neither men shared what happened the next day.

# Chapter 11

# Escape Route

When one is traveling in the direction, they search for themselves, it is not always an easy thing to accept that the way taken was not the right one. A lot of time one continues down that same stretch thinking eventually there will be clearing or markers to show the path taken was correct. Some will bypass turns and detours believing if they just stay the course eventually what they are seeking will be found. Some of those same people never return from that trip. Then there are those who find themselves going in that same direction, but after a lengthy ride passing turn around points, they eventually make the decision to look for the next exit point. Realizing the road would not lead them to where they had initially planned to go. Those few are survivors and that one decision to accept they were wrong finally sunk in. After that day in the office with my manager, the physical abuse was no more, but the mental had not changed. There was a vibe of hostility, but an unspoken awareness that acknowledged physical torment would not be recommended. In honesty, I believe the fact he would not touch me caused the hostility to grow in the way that it did and motivated the drinking to be worst then before. After a couple months, I just could not get ahead in this town and the unhappiness I felt with this man was too powerful to ignore anymore. My children had come down for the holidays, but how I felt was just too painful to ignore anymore. I wanted to go home, and I verbalized this without hesitation. We were no longer living in the "house" we originally came down for and I was not mad about that at all. Things fell through due to unkept promises and I was not willing to put money into something that was more of a burden to me than anything else. It only took me a few days to find a new place and I was relieved. To be honest, when I signed the lease and gave my deposit, I did not put his name nowhere on it. I did not hide this information from him either. This fact caused him to walk carefully, but I was not ignorant to the fact that he knew how to adapt. To show one thing while plotting something else. I had learned a lot dealing with this man. After a couple months past, the desire to leave had grown and I no longer wanted to experiment with the illusion that it could work. I had reached a point in my mind that I could care less if it did or did not with the preference of the latter. I began packing my things, my children things, and contacting the furniture company to pick up their stuff. I heard what my boyfriend was attempting to convince me with about us and this town. Even though I heard what he said, I did not agree with the thoughts spoken to me. This town held less than the one I was from with him and it made no sense to stay where I did not belong. The things I had went through in a few months with him in that town was enough to give the average person nightmares for the rest of their life. For me, I woke up from a long-drawn-outslumber and reality was setting in hard. I had developed a relationship with one of the cab drivers in that town and they also did extensive drives. I had planned with her a couple days before to return to my hometown with my children. I was excited and, on that day, I packed her trunk with our things, relieved. My first day out of slumber, I felt alive and ecstatic to be getting away from this man. I remember looking out the window at this big city for the last time, and felt no love lost for what it never gave me. I remember listening to my boyfriend laughing and talking with the driver. Looking at him, one would think he was just a regular man who loved to talk and joke. But if you watch closely, an abuser always presents the best to outsiders. That way when what they really are leaked out, doubt and disbelief would be the reaction towards the accusers. I remember studying him throughout that ride andbeing aware of how he felt nervous from my looks. At one point of time during the ride, I noticed the driver watching me in the rear-view mirror and knew without words she knew what the deal was without any words being exchanged. To me, it did not matter because every second that passed, I was closer to home with my babies. I remember seeing the sign for the town over to my hometown and excitement hit my heart. I was almost home! For so long, I had hated this town and now I could not wait to be back in it. The old saying is misery loves company. That was true, but if I had to live in misery I would rather do it from a place I already knew. I remember when the car turned into my mother's driveway and the pressure of tears building up within me. True it was my mother's house, but for me in that moment, I called it home. I had already informed my mom I was coming back, and she had left a way for me to get in. I remember my children jumping out happy to finally be out of the car and back on familiar grounds. Gathering my things and theirs, we piled everything into the living room until after I got things settled. Paying the driver, I remember hugging her and thanking her for everything. She responded by letting me know she was happy to have help, but mainly she was glad to get me out of a situation she saw was not good. It is amazing how people around you can see what you think they cannot. There was no hesitation with her looks, nor her words and I acknowledged for the first time this was true. I remember my boyfriend looking surprised that this was stated, and I agreed. I remember the driver looking at him and telling him there is not much that could fool her eyes from the things she has seen doing her job. He tried to laugh it off, but even I heard the fakeness and nervousness streaming from him for being put on the spot by someone he had just met. Walking the driver back out to her car, she made me promise to be happy and I did for what it was worth. At that point, my boyfriend informed me he would be going back with her to make sure the house was straight for the landlord. I was not surprised by what he had said and agreed that was good. Not because I knew that was really what he had planned, but because it meant time away from him that I was willing to give. I knew this was the separation I needed for the grip to end that he had. This was the way out I looked for and I had no intentions of letting this moment pass. Watching them leave, I exhaled a breath I had long been holding. I felt my shoulders drop in a relaxation I had not experienced in such a long time, but also was too nervous thinking he may change his mind. I stood there watching that car go back up the road we had just got off and I walked to the end of the driveway to be sure it kept going. When I saw the car top the hill out of my view, I remember throwing my head back gazing up at the sky and saying finally I am home. This had to be the new chapter for so many unhappy endings. It just had to be, please. Please.

# Chapter 12

# Soul Ties

Separation can bring about many different thoughts, reactions, and emotions depending on the situations. It can be damaging and cause mental strain or stress when this takes place. It can cause distress with endless waves of emotions to comprehend what has taken place for it to occur. It can cause temporary anxiousness while waiting for the moment when togetherness is once again experienced. Or it can cause absolute relief knowing everything connected with the situations are no longer present and missed. For me, the last is where I found myself when I saw my boyfriend leave out of my mother's yard going back to the town, I had no desire to see ever again. For me, the separation brought a lift that registered not just with my mind, but my atmosphere. I was at peace. Something I had not experienced but believed that this what I was feeling at the time was truly what it was. For two weeks, I walked around feeling this way after returning home. There was this moment, this space, that was new to me and I was grateful for it for the first time. I remember the desire to keep this space and fight to not lose it. There was this desperation that had begun to build in me the more I experienced this unknown freedom. Each night, I laid my head down without fear or nervousness that the person lying beside me would attempt to harm me in some form or fashion. I did not have to guard my looks and I wake up each morning not feeling drained just to open my eyes to another day of pure bitterness. It was not a battle for me just to be me for those few precious moments, but everything would eventually come to an end. I remember during my peace time my boyfriend still managed to call and "check" on me as he liked to put it. During those calls I would sometimes sit on the phone just staring at the receiver and barely said sentences in response to his comments. After a few days of being out of his presence, I started ignoring his calls and barely responded to texts. Thinking back to those times, I almost felt as if a haze was lifting off my mind, the longer I was away from him. With him, he rarely stayed out of my space and I knew he was not liking the response he was getting from this separation. Little by little, the strings that netted me to him were snapping and I started recognizing the person I once knew again. Though she had many issues, at least there were some characteristics coming into focus of this person I once knew. For me, strength that had been slowly draining off me was being replaced and I felt it. I did little to hide this from him and during that first week of separation, I finally ended this death trap I knew was not a relationship. The second week of freedom was spent moving forward with some forms of getting my life back together. I was no longer drinking, and the taste was removed from my mouth by the time I was 24 years old. The smell of any type of alcoholic beverage caused my stomach to cringe and that was just fine with me. During my first two weeks home, my little cousin, who was like the little brother, was coming over with his small family almost nightly. It felt so good to have some form of normalcy without the strain of pretending. I remember one night during my second week home, my now ex-boyfriend, called while my family was at my mom's house. Hearing his voice, I did inform him I was busy and did not have time to talk. Now mind you, the confidence was building and building within me. So, moving on was the plan and moving without him was the goal. There was nothing in between this. Sounds easy right? Yes, I thought so too, but I forgot for a split moment the type of "person" I had become entangled with. I remember being asked who was at my mother's house and my answer was to inform him that was not his concern. After a few minutes of back and forth, I decided to end the call with a simple I must goI am leaving for the movies and hanging up the phone ending the debate that was attempting to come up. Going back to my family, we continued laughing and talking with our conversationsas we were leaving for the theater. I remember that this was the weekend that The Passion of The Christ came out and I really wanted to see it. I remember watching this movie and how my heart was torn with what I was witnessing. The very essence of this movie touched something inside of me that I did not realized was still there. I remember we all left the movies quiet and sober behind what we had just seen. There were no words, but we did manage to discuss each part and what it did to us.Later, after everyone had left, I made sure my children were in bed and prepared to rest for the night. My mother had gotten to the point where she was staying at my grandmother's next door due to her being up in age. So, my children and I basically had the house at that point which was comforting for me since I was not in my own at that time. I remember going to sit on the couch to watch a movie before going to bed that night at peace and happy for a fun evening with my little brother/cousin. I remember lying back on the couch watching whatever was on the television thinking about the movie we had just seen, but do not remember drifting off to sleep. There were those nights, even then, where the dark form I would see moving around would appear during that time. So, falling asleep on the couch was not something new to me, but it yet did not cause me to miss anything I had gone through up until that point. If I closed my eyes to it, I could pretend it was not there. I refused to let anything interrupt this feeling. I do not know how long I laid there asleep when I was awakened by force. I remember a hand across my mouth and something heavy holding me down. Jerked awake by this, my eyes opened to see my recent ex-boyfriend kneeling beside me with this crazed look on his face. I remember staring at him, afraid to move, trying to figure out how this man got into the house, and how no one knew he was there. Looking at me, he whispered and let me know just how easy it was for him to get to me. Standing up, he walked to the door, and left as if it was the most natural thing to do. I remember staring at the front door before getting up to lock it and running to grab a chair to place under the knob to block any unwanted entry. My heart was racing, my mind was struggling to figure out how, HOW, could I finally be free from the torture of one who was determined to strip me of me? I could feel the confines of the trap I had finally crawled out of laughing because of how amusing it was to see what I had come to accept be snatched out of my hands. Leaving a jagged cut as evidence that the hard battle I fought to escape this hole was useless and not mine to have. At that moment, for the first time, I heard the shadow form laugh in total glee that once again hopelessness was the dirty blanket comforting me. With a bowed head, once again the floor was my level of view.

# Chapter 13

# Whispers

Tone is a powerful tool used when it enters a conversation. Every person has one and utilizes it when they desire to get a point across, want to put emphasis on what they are saying, or simply want to be heard. Despite the way that it is used, it manages to always get its point across when it is applied. Depending on the situation itself, tone can set in motion whatever it wants for that specific time or moment it is used. If we think over past or recent experiences, we will see that whatever tone we initiated during the process brought about the reaction we either sought it to or brought about the expected (or not so expected) end to what it was connected to. Either way, the beginnings to the set tone can be identified as the applied pressure, we can say, for practically every moment we have connected to us and our walk-through life. But believe it or not, there is a certain tone that we all come to encounter at some point in our lives. Though some choose to ignore it, some choose to label it imagination, some choose to deny it, and some just block it out. The count can seem to be large when you add the previous sentence, it will not match the many who decide to listen when this tone presents itself. After that night of, what I considered, stalked terror I did not present the same tone I had come to feel confident in towards this man. I knew I had to some way somehow break free of him and at that point felt that if he moved on, it would bring about my freedom. As well as a safety I could not gain being in his company. I remember the next few days, him suddenly popping up at my mother's house practically every night. Even when I presented every excuse in the book to keep him from coming over, he still managed to show up as if I had said nothing. It got to the point that my little brother/cousin was starting to slack up in coming over due to him being over there. The loud and obnoxious way he presented himself did not fool my little cousin and I knew he was waiting for me to ask him for help. Knowing this, I could not and would not allow him to get mixed up in this. There was no way I would allow anything to happen and him pay for the foolish mistake I made for getting involve with someone like this. Though this man was an actor of many faces, there was a sadistic quality about him he hid behind a "cool person" mentality. I remember one night him calling on the phone, attempting to keep me occupied to where I could not talk to anyone else unless it was my children. The only way to keep him from showing up at that point was to stay on the phone with him. I did not trust him not to entermy home, harm me, and my children finding me the next morning. There were days I would find things moved around in my bedroom the next morning and I began to lose sleep from the uncomfortable atmosphere that was beginning. The way his mind work, I was beginning to learn, and I knew he felt if he could keep me connected through intercourse, I would stay. But where I was at that point, everything about him was causing a sickness that no medicine could help with and no amount of physical connection could distract. I could no longer walk around in this fog of delusion and I had no desire to enter back into that place. Even though I was battling with all these issues, I tried to keep my children from seeing what their mother was going through. I knew my children were growing up and it was difficult for my eldest not to see the truth. My daughter was showing signs of dislike and how she responded to him reflected her feelings. I realized that the poison I had breathed in being in this toxic relationship was now being inhaled by my children, especially my daughters. I remember one day saying to The Lord if you are there please help me out of this situation. The figure in black was closer than ever and made no bones in letting me know it was dwelling in the house with us. I remember one day my children had left for school and I decided not to go back to sleep due to feeling this presence surrounding me. I knew that I was being watched and whatever it was waited for me to close my eyes again now that I was alone. Even though I was relieved that this man did not come over the night before because of his binge drinking and drug use, (not surprising), the presence around me was darker. More dangerous than what rested on this man. I decided to stay up and just begin my morning with my daily chores. I had gotten to the point of showering with the curtain open because I would hear footsteps right outside the door and glancing in the hallway, no one would be there. Around early afternoon, I was just finishing cleaning the living room when I turned to go into the kitchen. Right when I walked past the hallway leading to the bedrooms, I saw this tall figure standing in the center of the hall. He was very slender with a black wide rim hat, long black coat, black boots, and black clothing. I remember stopping and glancing back down the hall only to see nothing there. I remember my heart pounding so hard in my chest to where I laid my hand on it trying to calm it down. After a moment, I walked over to the phone just to see if my mom was next door or at work. Learning she was at work, I hung up, looked down the hall again, and walked into the kitchen to prepare dinner for the kids to eat after they made it home. I remember pulling up pandora on my phone and finding a gospel song to listen to while I prepped my food at the sink. I do not remember the song that was playing at that moment, but I do remember the calm that came over me as I began to sing with the music. The distraction was welcomed, and it caused me to gently move out of that place of fear. I remember singing and enjoying the sound made from that song. Like a gentle rock that allowed me to see differently for a moment. Lately, I found myself being drawn to gospel music and I managed to play it every evening while my children did their schoolwork at the table or wherever they managed to be to complete it. While listening and singing, out of the corner of my eye I saw the same figure I had seen earlier in the hallway sitting on the end of the couch watching me. His legs were crossed, and his arms were crossed over his chest as if studying me in complete silence. I remember jumping and hollering out in shock when I noticed him. But once again when I turned to look, he was gone. At that point, I turned the music off and walked into the living room looking around. I looked down the hallway but could not go down it. For some reason I felt a fear that let me know not to walk down there. I knew if I had something would happen and I could feel the presence was building up with bolder attempts as if to let me know it was real. Turning to go back to the kitchen, while trying to convince myself it was not real, I heard a laugh that was light but eerily familiar. I remember looking around me attempting to see if my now re-established boyfriend had come into the house without me being aware of it. Calling out his name, there was no response and I turned to go back into the kitchen to finish my dinner. While standing at the sink, I started wondering if my mind had finally cracked under the stress of everything I was holding inside. Trying to comprehend what I thought I had saw, I heard a voice say very low "you will never escape me". Dropping my knife in the sink, I turned around thinking someone was behind me, but there was no one there. Running to the phone, I called my boyfriend and invited him over that night. It did not matter to me at that point who was over there with me and my children. I just could not be in there with my children alone. It is amazing how tone can set the moment in how it is being used and at that moment it was setting up much more than I could had ever thought or guessed.

# Chapter 14

# Missed Connection

Time has a way of reversing itself without a person truly understanding what is taking place. With the various changes every person experience, we do not always ponder over the time that has passed from day to day, season to season, or year to year. Once we do manage to consider that information, we realized that much time has been spent, but was there quality gained or lost. The answers towards that can range on various levels as well as thoughts. Several months had passed and the time was coming where I saw nothing but the barren wasteland of hope as my scenery. After that day at home alone, the dark figure was becoming a regular apparition seen daily and nightly at that point. I was beginning to barely give it a second glance when it appeared and did not try to block out the things it was whispering to me. For me, it was another uninvited guest who had made itself at home as this now undesired boyfriend I had. I remember one morning going through bags of clothes I had stored in the room my son slept in. For some reason, I decided to go through those things to see whether I still wanted what was in them. Pulling things out one by one, I remember pulling out my old aprons from the restaurant I had worked at before making that terrible move. Smiling I reached into the pockets only to find my tickets and papers still in them. Going through each paper, my hands stopped moving with one item in my hand. It was the card the man of God had given me and told me to contact him if I ever needed to talk. After all this time, that card was still in that apron pocket and at that precise moment I had it in my hand. I remember thinking should I try this number just to see if it were possible that he still had this number. Shaking my head, I decided not to even go there with false hope of finally speaking with someone who could help me. I remember packing my things back up, but that card stayed in my hand as I walked over to my dresser lying it down on it. Walking to the living room to turn on the radio, I went into the kitchen to prepare dinner for my children. It was Wednesday, my children had begun going to bible study at my old church, and I wanted to be sure they ate before attending. I remember looking outside and seeing how the sky was looking. It was obvious it was about to storm, so I was not sure if I were going to let them go or if church would still be that night. Either way dinner had to be completed and I turned my mind back to that. I remember checking my meat to find it was not quite ready and needed more time before I could do anything. Going back into the living room, I grabbed the remote to see what was on television. Though I was doing a channel surf to find something to help me pass time while waiting to cook, my mind fell on that little card on my dresser. I remember thinking it would not hurt to speak and decided to try the number just to see. I remember dialing the number and holding my breath not knowing what to expect. On the third ring, someone picked up and it was a female voice unfamiliar to me. Saying hello, I told the person who I was and asked if this was the number to the man of God I once knew. To my surprised, the woman acknowledged that it was and asked me to hold for a minute. The next voice I heard was one from my familiar past and the happiness I felt was immense. Asking him could he recognize my voice, to my amazement he did! I remember the happiness slowly transferring over to tears to hear his voice once again. I believe he heard my sniffing because he got quite before asking me to share with him what was wrong. Before I could stop myself, everything poured out of my mouth like a faucet and I could not stop myself from sharing practically everything. He sat listening, never interrupted me, but listened without making a noise. When I finished talking, I remember him say "Jesus" and proceeded to talk to me. I remember in that first portion of his words, he asked me was I still going to church, and I told him no. He did not fuss, nor did he get upset, just continued talking to me like a father to his daughter. I remember sharing with him that I did send my children to bible study because they asked me could they go, and I did not to deny them that. He told me he was proud of me for this and continued talking to me. I remember him asking me was I still dreaming and seeing things before they happened. I informed him that I was, and they were getting worse. He positioned to me that after my children left talk to God and just listened to what He had to say. At that moment, I wanted to tell him I have been talking to Him, but He does not say anything back to me. I wanted to share that with him, but I did not. Agreeing to do what he asked me to do. After our conversation, the man of God prayed for me and told me to keep in touch with me agreeing to do just that. Hanging up, I felt a relief to have spoken to someone and went back to the kitchen to finish cooking. A couple hours later my children were home from school, and I prepared their plates for dinner. It started storming not long after they came into the house, so I was not sure bible study would be taking place for them to go. A little after 6 PM that evening, the storm slacked up and the van was outside blowing to pick them up. Watching them climb into the van excited for church, I smiled because it was a wonderful feeling to see the excitement they had for church. Closing the door, I remember looking around the house thinking I had to be in it alone for a couple more hours at night. Thinking on the conversation I had with the man of God, I considered what he had instructed me to do concerning listening to God. So, I decided okay I will try again, but this time do it the way the man of God had told me to do it. Turning the television off, I sat down on the couch in front of the living room windows. Putting my back to the outside while facing the interior of the house with no chance of turning my back to not see what was going on in that house. Leaning back, I remember looking up at the ceiling and saying "ok, God, I am listening. What do You want to say?" Leaning my head back against the couch while closing my eyes, I remember everything becoming silent and still. Suddenly rain drops hitting a bucket on the porch caught my attention and my mind began to focus on that sound. Listening to it, I knew the bucket was on the far corner of the porch because that is where it normally was, and the sound became almost mesmerizing. The next thing I knew, the sound was getting closer and soon it was as the bucket was directly behind the window I was sitting in front of. Suddenly I heard this voice speak to me over the sound of the rain drops hitting this bucket. The voice said, "I'm this close (referencing the drops of rain hitting the bucket), you are this far away (suddenly the rain drops on the bucket sounded from the yard a distance from the window!) meet Me halfway." I remember jumping up off the couch breathing fast and very hard. I ran to the window to look on the porch and saw the bucket in its normal spot there. Closing the door, I remember looking around and saying that did not just, yet I knew that it had. Running to the phone, I called the man of God to tell him what happened, and he laughed as if it was not a surprised. I remember him saying to me "so are you going to answer His call" and my mind understanding clearly what was being asked of me without any confusion. I remember a voice speak inside of me telling me the call was for me to acknowledge. I had a choice. Hanging up with the man of God, I felt this wondrous feeling rising in me and a curiosity that God wanted me for something? Really? I remember while standing there in my thoughts, the front door opened, and my mom walked into the house. Letting me know she had come to grab something before heading over to my grandmother for the night. Standing there, I stopped her and told her I believe God had just called me to do something for Him. Looking at her with excitement, I really wanted to hear what she had to say. Maybe because of everything I had done, and the many disappointments caused her reaction to not reflect the hope that I was wanting from her. I remember the crush behind her reaction, so once again I closed my heart and accepted the shelter of darkness as well as isolation to ever belong or receive anything good on this earth.

# Chapter 15

# Pruned Tree

Years go by and for every person there are one or more that can be remembered due to events that took place. Each year represents more than the number assigned to it, but also the moments set in motion that were particularly assigned to them. With each year is also the pattern of seasons and it is in those timings we associated memories like programs. Mass amount of people have a certain season they love much more than the others because of what is affiliated to it. Few find any to all to dislike, but for one who can see things before they happened, it is different for them. The year 2007 came in as any other, but there were seasons that were assigned for purpose that would not be delayed nor stop. I remember beginning this year knowing that I would not end it with this man. There was no pretense of any form of emotional ties and no attempts to "rekindle" a flame where the logs were completely burned out with no way to be relit. Even if there were extra logs to help assist with a fire, I had long ago tossed the matches away and dumped water over the excess logs to make them unusable. There was no doubt in my mind, he knew this was the case and nothing he could do up until that point was working. Even his manipulative actions and sadistic ways was not enough to cage me back to that place I had escaped previously. After that encounter in the living room with God and the response from my mom, my emotional state was a I do not care at all mannerism supported by a wall. Even though I presented this, it did not have a stance within my dreams at night. I continued to dream, and dream, and dream with a steadiness that felt as if it would not stop. That particular year, my grandmother eating habits were gradually leaving. I remember going over to her house to check on her and noticing that the food I had started bringing over she was not eating. My grandmother and I had a strange relationship, but for some reason we always manage to make each other laugh. This was a woman I had known all my life, so I knew her habits from the many times we were in each other company. I remember moving away and dreaming of my grandmother one night. Waking up the next day, I called her to check on her and she asked me to come home she needed me. My grandmother had never said anything like that to me before but hearing her say that and dreaming on her the night before, I went home to see about her. I was still in contact with the man of God and enjoyed our conversation when I got the chance to speak with him. I avoided calling that much because he always managed to ask about that encounter with God, but never pushed me to see what happened after speaking with him regarding what was said. I was glad for this because sobriety had hit me like an avalanche and the special moment became a painful thought, so to the back of my mind it went. I remember in the month of May in the year of 2007, I had a dream that shook me to the core and caused me to wake up hollering. I remember grabbing my phone and texting my little cousin/brother telling him I had just had this dream. I remember he text me back and promised he would be out there that night. Lying back down, my heart felt very heavy and nothing I could do would shake it off. That night my cousin came over with his family and I told them the dream. He was during that time the only one who knew I had dreams like that and never criticized or made fun of me when I told him. After talking about it and not knowing what it meant, we started talking about other things. None of us knew that one dream carried seasons within it. Before they left, I remember my cousin sharing that his wife's grandfather was sick. He was a well-respected and loved person in our family and within the small community we were from. We were hopeful everything would be okay, and he would bounce back like he had done before. I remember locking the door behind them while thinking about what he had just shared with me about his wife's grandfather. I remember thinking how this man reminded me greatly of my grandfather and I prayed that she would be spared how I felt from my loss a while longer. This was my hope for her, but I had come to associated nothing positive to my dreams which this one counted as one. A few nights later, I remember having another dream and when I opened my eyes, I already knew what it meant. I reached over grabbed my phone to text my cousin what I had saw. We agreed for them to come out that night again so that his wife could laugh and enjoy herself. I knew from my dream her family would have a great loss and later that night, after they left, her grandfather passed away. I remember her texting me and telling me what I dreamed happened but thanked me for that night of fun. I let her know we were family but did not feel that I deserved to be thanked for being the bearer of news like that. I remember considering dreams I had of things like this before connected to family, friends, and strangers. It never got easier seeing these things and it would not get any easier moving forward. June came in like it always does following the month of May, but that one dream was still hanging around just as strong as it was when I first had it. The first week of this month, I had a dream concerning my eldest uncle that caused me to wonder why I would see him. I refused to think anything and felt dread creeping closer and closer as the day moved forward. The next day, my family was contacted to let us know my eldest uncle was hospitalized. I remember wanting to go with my family to see him, but due to my children having school I could not. Watching them leave, the dream I had shared with my cousin came into my thoughts and that feeling of dread began moving over me. Pushing it backwards, I began saying confident things that went opposite of what I was feeling. One night, I was watching television with my children and boyfriend when the phone rang. I knew it was my mom calling because she was keeping me posted on my uncle's condition. I had already made plans to go back with them to see him when they came back in a day or two. Answering the phone to my mother's voice, I asked how he was doing. "He's gone, Keshia" were the words I received after asking. I remember crying out in denial while weeping I never got to tell him goodbye. I could not understand this portion of my life. Why those I love left before I could say goodbye. My mom was talking to me over the phone, but her words were lost in pain and grief. Hanging up the phone, I attempted to gain comfort from my boyfriend but quickly realized something one does not have they cannot give. So that night my comfort was my tears and the dream I had of my beloved uncle a few nights before. The next few weeks were a blur for me, but I could not stay there because of the attention my grandmother was needing. It was a primary duty to be sure she was okay and try to figure out what was going on. I also wanted to check in with the man of God since I had missed our normal week of wise conversation. I remember calling him in the month of August and apologizing for missing our schedule date. I remember him saying it was fine and asking how everything had been going. I had shared with him my uncle's death, cousin's grandfather's death, and my grandmother's appetite change concerns during one of our past conversations, so I filled him in on other things. I remember sharing that dream from June with him and telling him how I could not shake it. At that moment, he began to share an experience he had the prior week with me, and I remembered being wowed by it. Not because he shared it, but because he trusted me to tell me and it sounded so like my experiences. After ending our conversation, I gave my word that I would not miss our schedule call and made him promise that he and his wife would come to my wedding when the date came. I remember him laughing and saying they would not miss it for anything, before hanging up. That was a promise I intended to see happen.

# Chapter 16

# Set Time

No matter what anything looks like or sounds like, there is a purpose for everything to take place. We made not understand nor realize it during those times, but we can believe there is assigned dates predestined for everything including everyone. Letting go is not an easy thing to do especially when you have come to be used to a person, place, or thing being there every moment it is sought. It is in those moments when it is no longer present that we realized that nothing, absolutely nothing, in this world last that is connected to this human form. When realization sets in surrounding this truth, it becomes even more important to make those lasting memories worthwhile and letting go of the past experiences. We only get one shot to give a person their flowers and the importance of that has sunk in for me in this hour.

My grandmother did not seem to be getting better when it came to eating. For some reason or the other she just simply refused to do it. No amount of begging, coercing, or even showing anger was working at this point, so trying to figure out what was going wrong was an immediate reaction. I remember thinking about this one morning when suddenly I heard a voice whisper something to me. With my eyebrows raised, I googled what had entered my thoughts and found that the symptoms were like practically the same. Calling my aunt, who lived out of town, I presented that information to her and she agreed for me to discuss this with her doctor when I took her to her next appointment. I had basically become my grandmother's shadow when everyone was gone during the day. I remember taking my grandmother to her appointment and presenting the information I had found that seemed to outline what was going on with her. Listening to my thoughts, the doctor agreed to do a test and setup a new appointment to determine whether what I was thinking could possibly be the issue. I remember being surprised this doctor did not shut down my theories but was willing to investigate even to simply give me peace. A few weeks later, I brought my grandmother to this new appointment to complete the test for my concerns. Later we were informed that what had fell in my thoughts weeks prior was the situation. I remember the shock and disbelief in hearing this. Not understanding how I could have known to present this to not just my family but also her doctor. Even though I could not understand this, I was still grateful that my family had an answer to our concerns. Surgery was schedule and we prepared to once again see a healthy matriarch moving around like she once did. I remember one night, not long before her surgery was schedule having another one of my dreams. In this one I saw my grandmother, but she looked like the person she was prior to her refusal to eat. Waking up, I remember thinking I will not consider anything remotely negative concerning this dream and of her situation. My aunt had come home, so I did not have to go and be with her majority of the day like I had been doing. It was the weekend and I needed to do some things around the house before my aunt left returning home. I remember the phone ringing and upon answering it hearing my aunt's voice on the other end asking me to come over quick. Walking next door, I remember hearing my grandmother moaning from the den area and going to see what was going on. I remember seeing my grandmother sitting on the sofa rubbing her side as if she were in tremendous pain. My aunt asked me to look at my grandmother's side and see if it looked swollen to me. I remember asking my grandmother to lift her hand and saw that it was extended in a swollen manner. Hearing this, my aunt decided to take my grandmother to the hospital, and I went back to my mom's house. Cleaning that day, my mind could not focus on much being concerned about what was going on. My grandmother and I had a strained relationship, but these past few months were the best we had ever had. She had shared many things with me, and I found out she loved to laugh. Later, that day, I was told my grandmother was being transferred to another facility in a different town. That made no sense to me and at that moment, I could not get a clear understanding towards what was going on. Only it was serious, and the transfer was needed for her to receive the assistance she required. A couple days later, I had another dream and this time I saw my deceased uncle and my grandmother in the same house. Waking up, I remember lying in the bed crying. There was no denying what I was being told and I could no longer ignore what I was seeing. A day later, I remember being told what the situation was and just listened to the confirmation of what I had dreamed. My grandmother was sent home and was made comfortable for the time she had left. On the morning she left, I remember waking up and looking towards her house before getting up to go to the restroom. Lying back down, before my head touch the pillow, the phone to the house rang and my mother answered it. I heard her get up and move around in her room. There was no need to get up and ask what was going on when I already knew. I remember my mom coming to my bedroom letting me know my grandmother was gone and me simply saying I know. Later that day, the stress of my grandmother's passing, my uncle's passing, and my life was a pressure that was just too much to carry. The dreams were just too much to take, but there was no one who could take them away from me. That night I called the most familiar person to me at that time for something, just something. Calling my boyfriend, I asked him to please come get me and explained what was going on. I remember this man asking me what I wanted him to do and my mouth dropping in complete disbelief. I remember saying never mind enjoy your night and hanging that phone up with him for the final time. I knew that once I hung that phone up, it was the end of an era I would no longer entertain or acknowledge. I not only lost my grandmother that day, but a time stamp had formally sealed the end of an invisible chapter I was unknowingly a part of. Though the chapters were long,and the plot was intense, the truth of the matter was, it was just beginning. After that night, my now ex-boyfriend attempted many things to get me back. The passing of my grandmother was enough to sever any ties within my mind that would assist in the delusion that there was anything left. 2007 was a year that brought about a transitional period that I was happy to leave and even more happy to limit thoughts. Coming into 2008, it was not an easy period for me. I did not celebrate a new year and I did not have any resolutions to look forward too. The only things that kept me focused was my children, these strange gifts, and my attempts to understand what was going on with me. I was still speaking with the man of God, but my grief in all the loss from the year before was causing me to separate from people. I realized how quickly things could change and I could not go through that again. Caring for people simply hurt too much. I remember the man of God contacting me one day in August of this new year. He let me know he had been concerned for me and knew I was angry with God. There was no point in asking how he knew this, he managed to know a lot of things without me saying anything. Listening to him, I wanted to believe that life was not given to me for me to feel like a punching bag, but the hits I was taken did not seem that way. Being standoffish was my way of protecting myself and I did not see any other way to avoid pain. I gave my word to him, I would not turn away from God, but never uttered how I felt God had turned away from me. Giving my word I would keep our monthly meeting, I hung up feeling just as lost as I had always felt. I remember missing the week of our call due to me receiving my old employment back. I remember calling the man of God the following week with my happy news, but his tone was different this time. Normally the cheerful person who discussed scriptures with me and encouraged me sounded different to my ears. Asking was he alright, I remember him sharing an experience he had just had and how he could not forget it. Listening to him, I remember asking would he ever come back to my hometown to preach again? Possible starting another church and my giving my word I would attend to sit under him to learn. Though I was pushing away from people again, I knew this man of God was the only one who could explain what was going on with me as far as the dreams and visions. I remember him laughing and saying wherever The Lord sends him he would go. Speaking for a moment longer, I remember telling him thank you for helping me understand about what I am going through. I gave him my word I would continue to move forward. Hanging up, I remember a feeling I could not shake, but pushed it to the back of my thoughts. Suddenly the dream I had the following year came into my thoughts, but I refuse to acknowledge it. The following weeks, I never got a call back from the man of God and I never would. I remember having a dream and seeing the man of God preaching with sweat falling off him like rain. I remember him ending what he was saying, turning to me, smiling, and walking away. A few days later, I received a call informing me the man of God I had come to consider my mentor and friend had passed away. I remember sitting down on the couch and staring out into the yard at my mother's house. Death seemed to desire those close to me and at that moment, I stood waiting at the door. Living, to me by then, was just not fair but the wheels for it had only just begun to turn.

# Dedications

First and foremost,
I would like to give honor to the
Highest God. Because of His hand being upon my life, I would not be here. Because of His grace and mercy, I would not have a story to tell. I thank you Father, for every breath you have allowed to enter my lungs to tell that miracles still happen daily.
To my grandfather and grandmother,
the seed started through your connections and The Lord ordaining for you to meet each other. Never have I witness the strength of two individuals that dripped down upon the products of this union. Granddaddy, you were more than just a grandfather. You were the first man here on this earth that showered me with a natural love from your heart. You went out of your way for all that knew you and left a story for everyone who encounter you. Your physical form left when I was young, but your presence has never left my heart.
I will forever love you, Granddaddy.
To my mother,
there is not a day that you do not demonstrate strength and endurance. You have been a hard worker all my life and I admire you for this.

Thank you for the passion to read that you passed onto me. Through that passion, a dream of becoming an author has blossomed to come forth. I love you to infinity and thank you for everything you have done.
Sincerely,
Keshia

www.ingramcontent.com/pod-product-compliance
Lightning Source LLC
Chambersburg PA
CBHW062039120526
44592CB00035B/1527